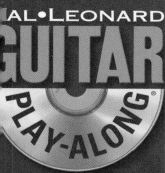

CONTENTS

Cover photo: © Krister Nyman / Scanpix / Retna

Tracking, mixing, and mastering by
Jake Johnson & Bill Maynard at Paradyme Productions
All guitars by Doug Boduch
Bass by Tom McGirr
Keyboards by Warren Wiegratz
Drums by Scott Schroedl

ISBN 978-1-4234-6984-1

HAL•LEONARD®
CORPORATION

7777 W. BLUEMOUND RD. P.O. BOX 13819 MILWAUKEE, WI 53213

Cry, Cry, Cry

Words and Music by John R. Cash

*Symbols in parentheses represent chord names respective to capoed guitar.
Symbols above reflect actual sounding chords. Capoed fret is "0" in tab.

1. Ev-'ry-bod-y knows _ where you go when the sun _ goes down.
2., 3., 4. *See additional lyrics*

_ I think you on - ly live _ to see the lights _

Chorus

5

⊕ **Coda**

Outro

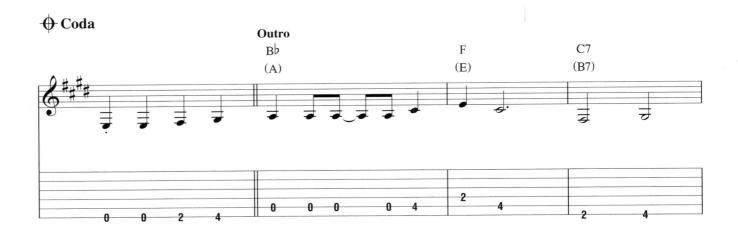

Additional Lyrics

2. Soon your sugar daddies will all be gone.
   You'll wake up some cold day and find you're alone.
   You'll call for me but I'm gonna tell you bye, bye, bye.
   When I turn around and walk away you'll cry, cry, cry.

3. I lie awake at night to wait till you come in.
   You stay a little while and then you're gone again.
   Ev'ry question that I ask I get a lie, lie, lie.
   For ev'ry lie you tell you're gonna cry, cry, cry.

4. When your fickle love gets old no one will care for you.
   Then you'll come back to me for a little love that's true.
   I'll tell you no, and then you'll ask me, "Why, why, why?"
   When I remind you of all of this you'll cry, cry, cry.

Chorus   You're gonna cry, cry, cry and you'll want me then.
   It'll hurt when you think of the fool you've been.
   You're gonna cry, cry, cry.

I Walk the Line

Words and Music by John R. Cash

Capo I

*Symbols in parentheses represent chord names respective to capoed guitar.
Symbols above reflect actual sounding chords. Capoed fret is "0" in tab.

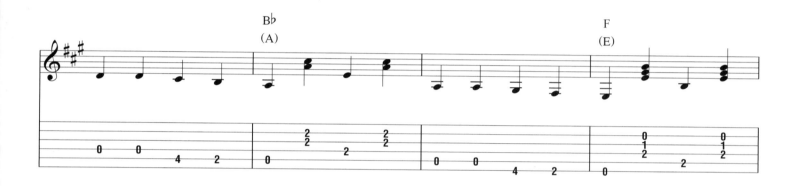

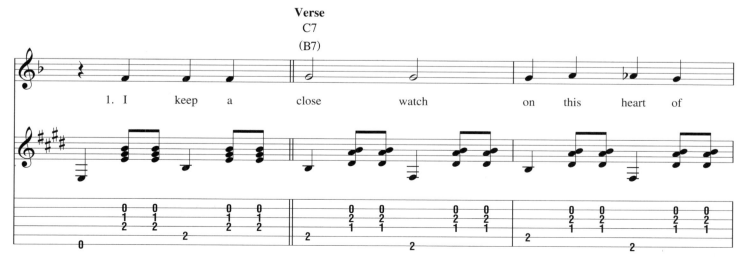

1. I keep a close watch on this heart of

Verse

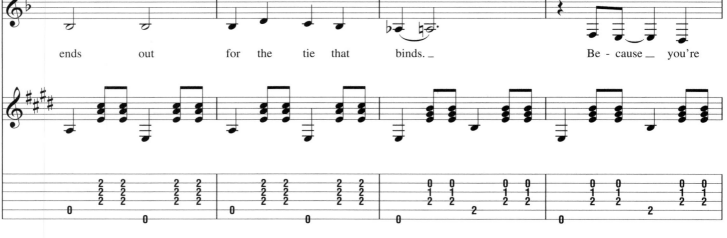

Additional Lyrics

4. You've got a way to keep me on your side.
   You give me cause for love that I can't hide.
   For you I know I'd even try to turn the tide.
   Because you're mine, I walk the line.

Folsom Prison Blues

Words and Music by John R. Cash

Capo I

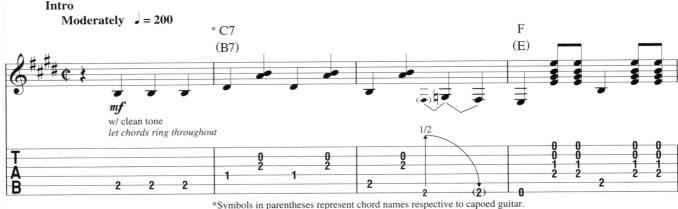

*Symbols in parentheses represent chord names respective to capoed guitar.
Symbols above reflect actual sounding chords. Capoed fret is "0" in tab.

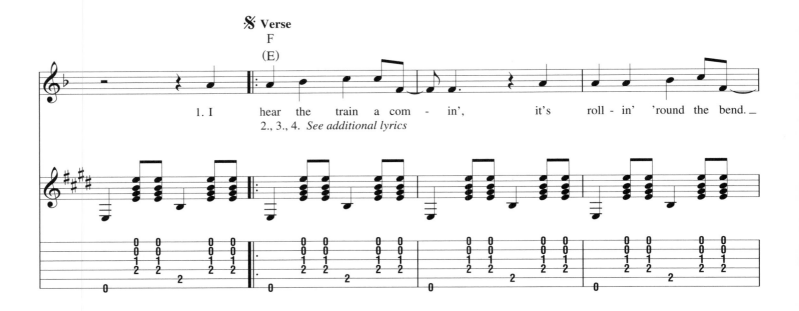

1. I hear the train a com - in', it's roll - in' 'round the bend. __
2., 3., 4. *See additional lyrics*

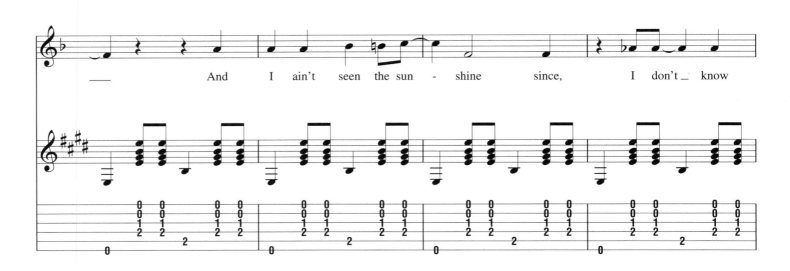

__ And I ain't seen the sun - shine since, I don't __ know

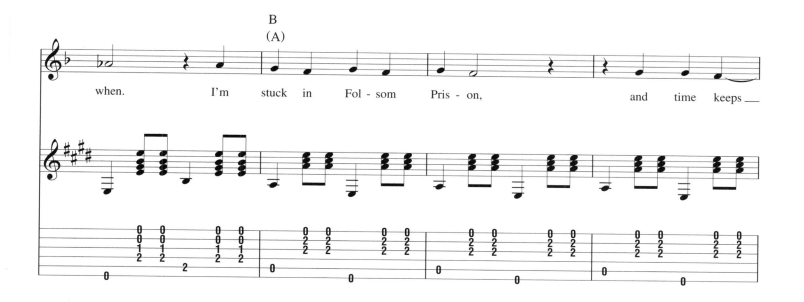

B
(A)

when.   I'm stuck in Fol - som Pris - on,   and time keeps ___

F
(E)

___ drag - gin' on.

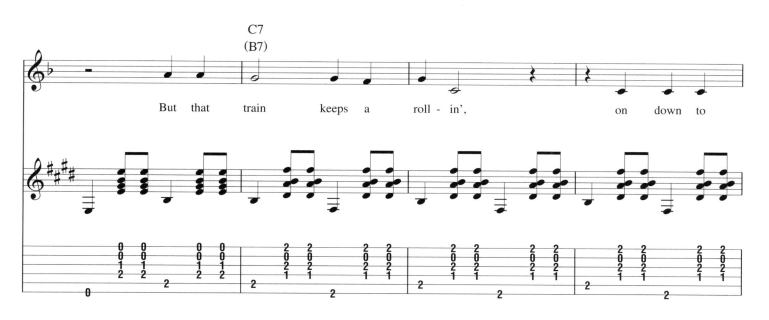

C7
(B7)

But that train keeps a roll - in',   on down to

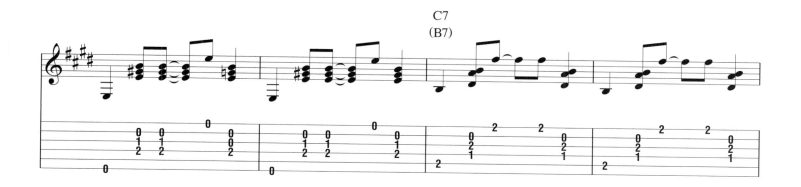

1st time, D.S.
(take 2nd ending)
2nd time, D.S. al Coda

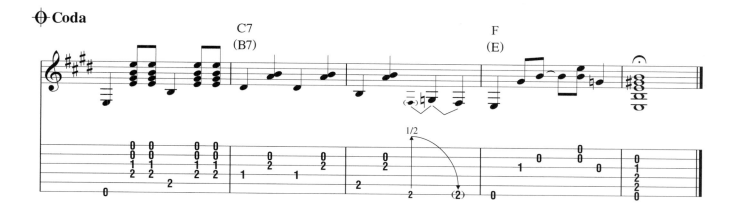

Additional Lyrics

2. When I was just a baby, my mama told me son,
   Always be a good boy; don't ever play with guns.
   But I shot a man in Reno just to watch him die.
   When I hear that whistle blowin' I hang my head and cry.

3. I bet there's rich folk eatin' in a fancy dining car.
   They're prob'ly drinkin' coffee and smokin' big cigars.
   But I know I had it comin', I know I can't be free.
   But those people keep a movin', and that's what tortures me.

4. Well, if they freed me from this prison, if that railroad train was mine,
   I bet I'd move it on a little farther down the line,
   Far from Folsom Prison, that's where I want to stay.
   And I'd let that lonesome whistle blow my blues away.

Jackson

Words and Music by Billy Edd Wheeler and Jerry Leiber

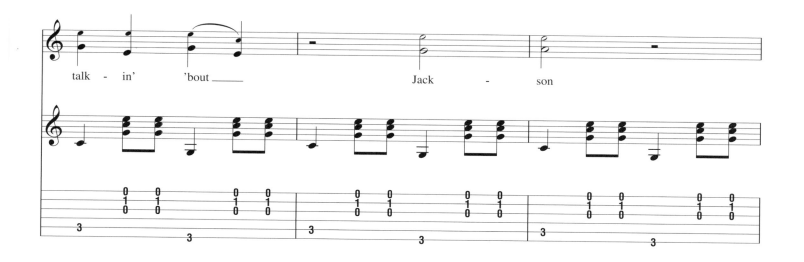

talk - in' 'bout _____ Jack - son

2nd time, substitute Fill 1
3rd time, substitute Fill 3

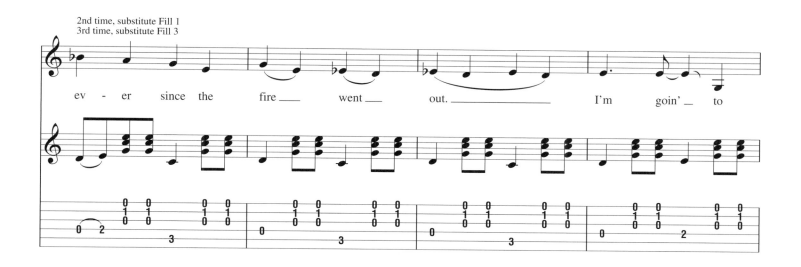

ev - er since the fire _____ went _____ out. _____ I'm goin' _ to

Fill 1

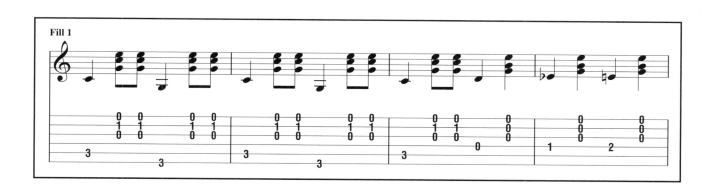

Fill 3

Jack - son, _ go 'head _ and wreck your _____

health. _ Go play your _____ hand, you _____

2nd time, substitute Fill 2

big talk - in' man, and make _ a big fool of _____ your -

Fill 2

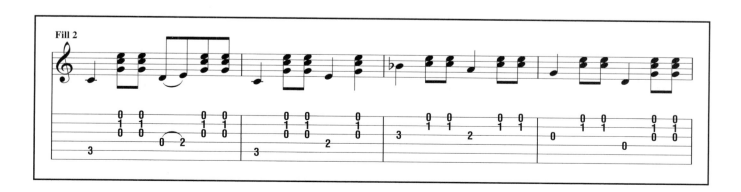

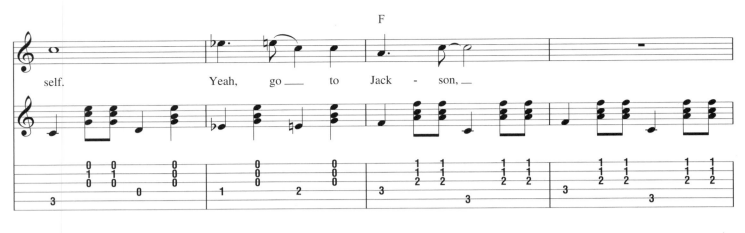

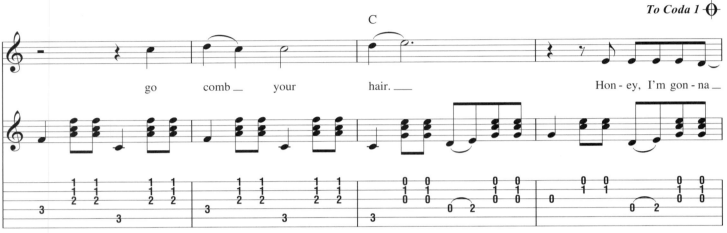

To Coda 1 ⊕

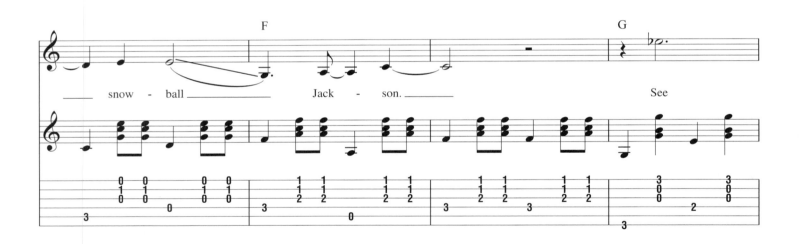

⊕ Coda 1

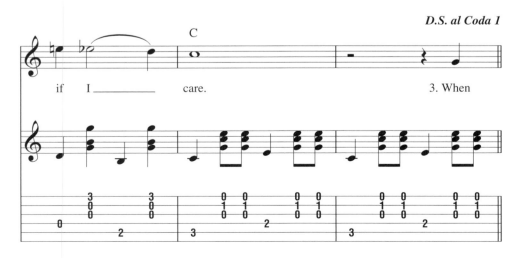

22

D.S. al Coda 2

Coda 2

Outro

23

Mm. ___
hot - ter than ___ a pep - per

Begin fade

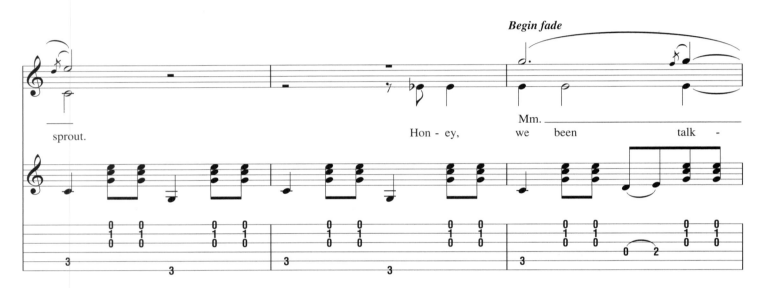

sprout.

Mm. ___
Hon - ey, we been talk -

Fade out

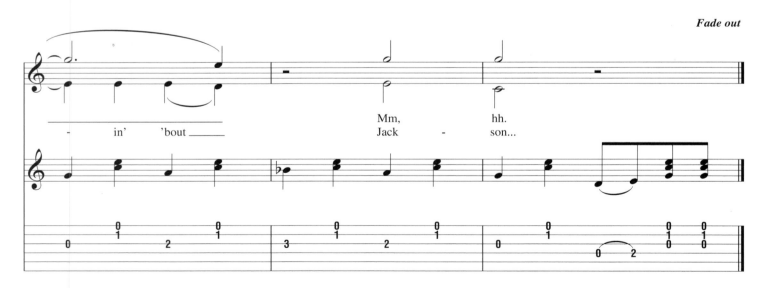

- in' 'bout ___

Mm, hh.
Jack - son...

Additional Lyrics

3. When I breeze into that city,
   People gonna stoop and bow.
   All them women gonna make me
   Teach 'em what they don't know how.
   I'm goin' to Jackson,
   You turn a, loose a, my coat,
   'Cause I'm goin' to Jackson.
   "Goodbye," that's all she wrote.

4. But they'll laugh at you in Jackson,
   And I'll be dancin' on a pony keg.
   They'll lead you 'round town like a scalded hound
   With your tail tucked between your legs.
   Yeah, go to Jackson,
   You big talkin' man.
   And I'll be waitin' in Jackson
   Behind my Japan fan.

5. Mm, well, now, we got married in a fever,
   Hotter than a pepper sprout.
   We been talkin' 'bout Jackson
   Ever since the fire went out.
   I'm goin' to Jackson,
   And that's a fact.
   Yeah, we're going to Jackson,
   Ain't never comin' back.

The Man in Black

Words and Music by John R. Cash

Capo III

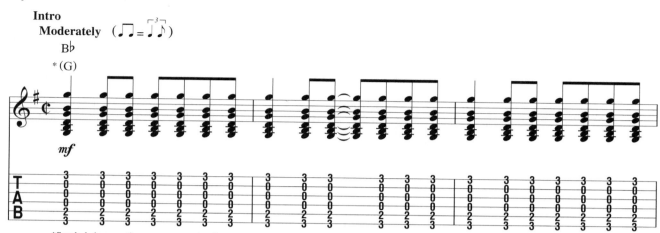

*Symbols in parentheses represent chord names respective to capoed guitar.
Symbols above reflect actual sounding chords. Capoed fret is "0" in tab.

1. Well, you won-der why___ I al-ways dress in___
2., 4. *See additional lyrics*

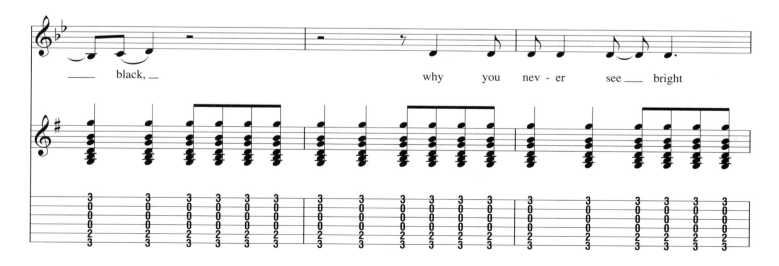

___ black, ___ why you nev-er see ___ bright

⊕ Coda

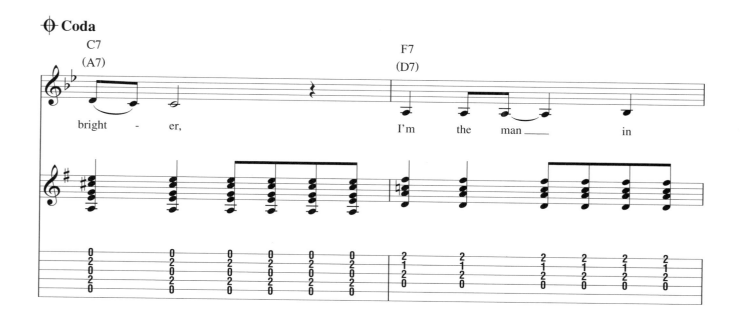

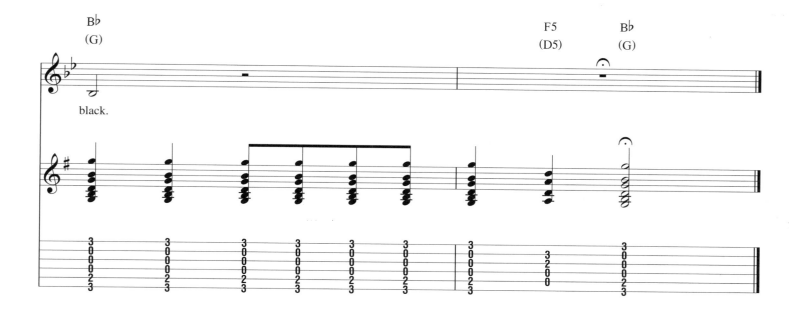

Additional Lyrics

2. I wear the black for those who've never read,
   Or listened to the words that Jesus said
   About the road to happiness through love and charity.
   Why you'd think He's talkin' straight to you and me.
   Well, we're doin' mighty fine, I do suppose,
   In our streak of lightnin' cars and fancy clothes.
   But just so we're reminded of the ones who are held back,
   Up front there ought to be a man in black.

4. Well, there's things that never will be right, I know
   And things need changin' ev'rywhere you go.
   But till we start to make a move to make a few things right,
   You'll never see me wear a suit of white.
   Aw, I'd love to wear a rainbow ev'ry day
   And tell the world that ev'rything's O.K.
   But I'll try to carry off a little darkness on my back.
   Till things are brighter, I'm the man in black.

Orange Blossom Special

Words and Music by Ervin T. Rouse

Intro
Moderately ♩ = 112
Double-time feel

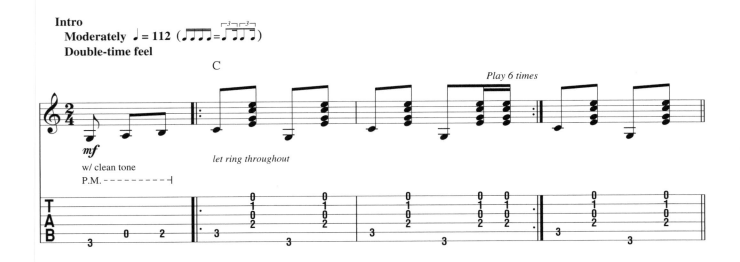

let ring throughout
w/ clean tone
P.M.

𝄋 **Verse**

1. Look a yon - der com - in',   com - in' down ___ that
2., 3. *See additional lyrics*

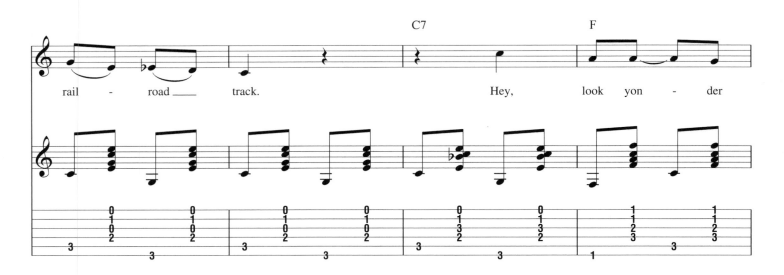

rail - road ___ track.   Hey,   look yon - der

com - in',　　　　　　　　com - in' down ___ that rail - road ___

C　　　　　　　　　　　　　　　G7

track.　　　　　It's　　the　Orange　Blos - som　Spe - cial

To Coda 2 ⊕

Interlude
C

bring - in' ___ my ba - by ___ back.

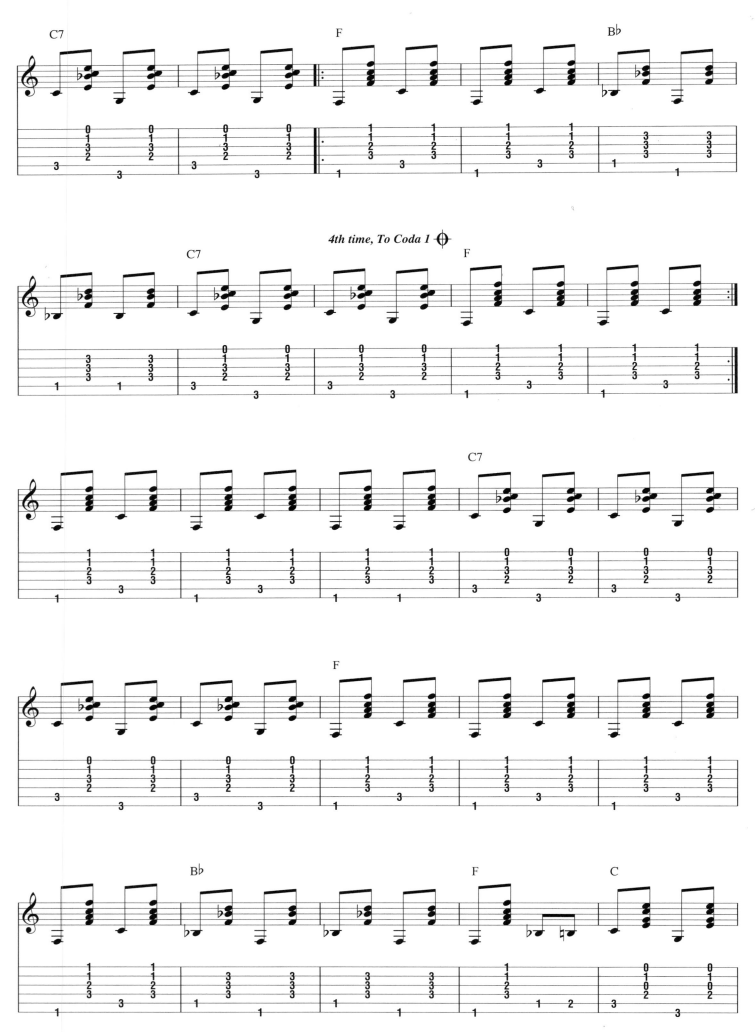

4th time, To Coda 1

34

D.S. al Coda 2   ⊕ **Coda 2**

Outro

Begin fade

Fade out

Additional Lyrics

2. Well, I'm goin' down to Florida and get some sand in my shoes.
   Or maybe California and get some sand in my shoes.
   I'll ride that Orange Blossom Special and lose these New York Blues.

3. He talk about a ramblin', she's the fastest train on the line.
   Talk about a trav'lin', she's the fastest train on the line.
   It's that Orange Blossom Special rollin' down the seaboard line.

Ring of Fire

Words and Music by Merle Kilgore and June Carter

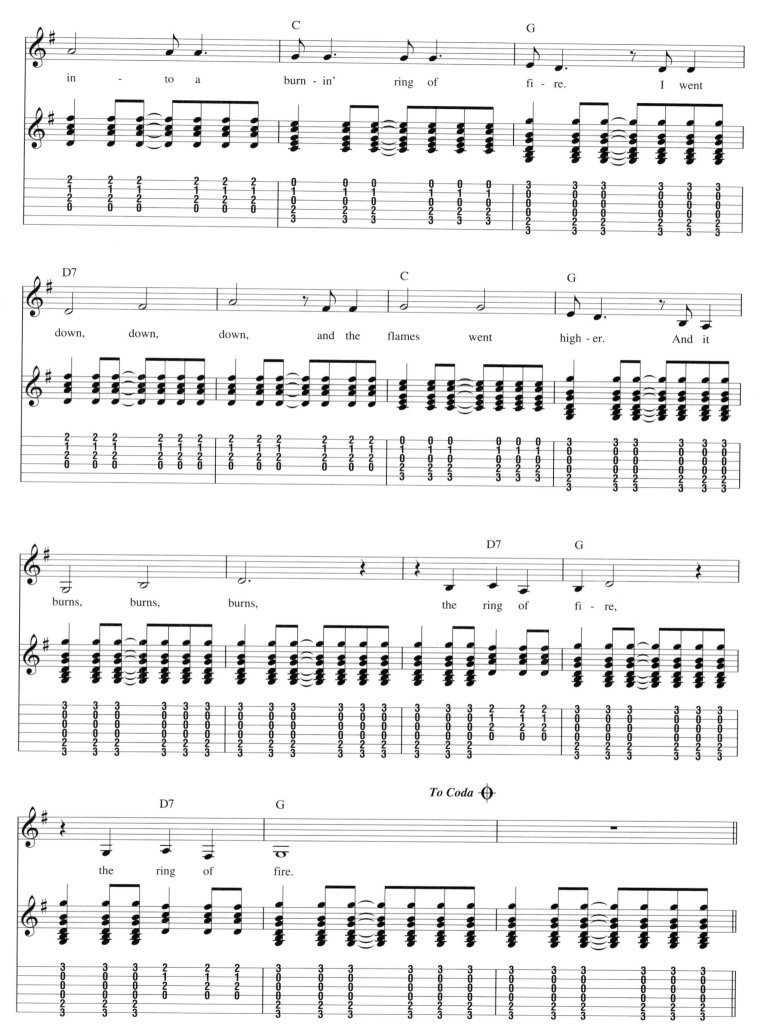

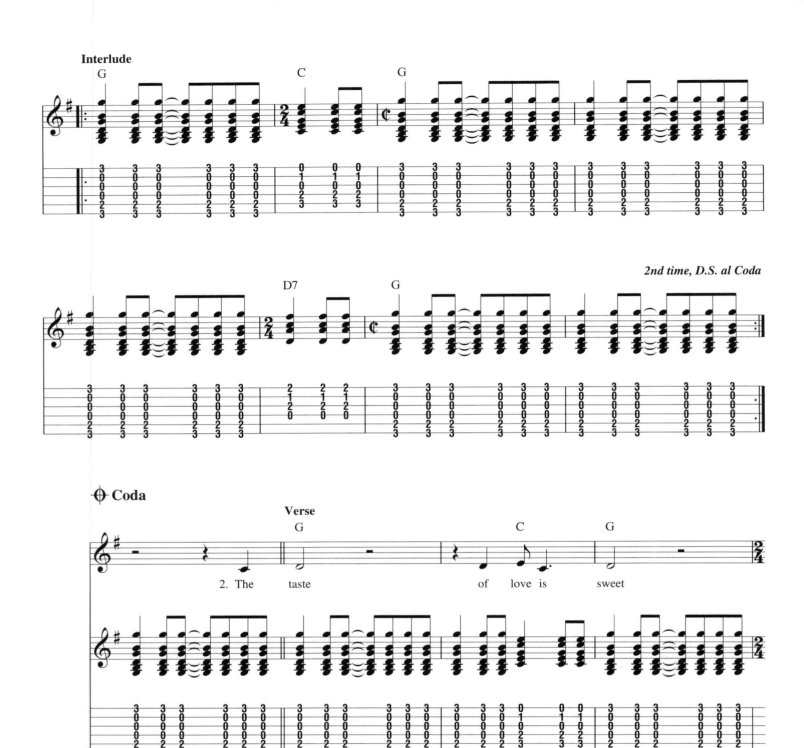

2nd time, D.S. al Coda

Coda

2. The taste of love is sweet

when hearts

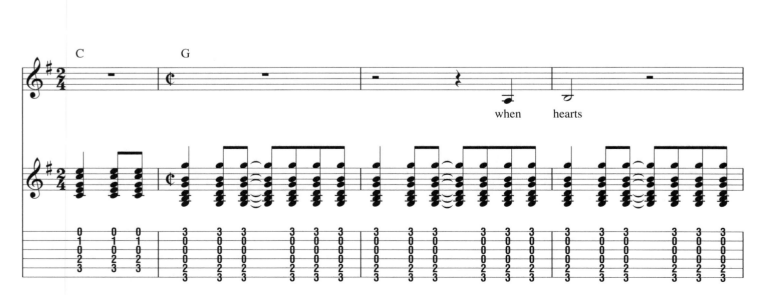

Chorus

Tennessee Flat Top Box

Words and Music by Johnny Cash

Capo I

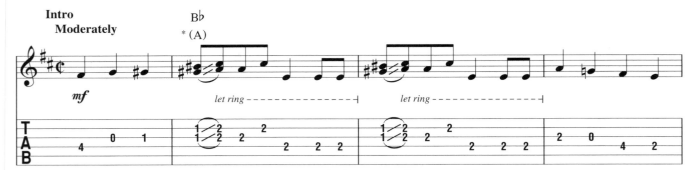

*Symbols in parentheses represent chord names respective to capoed guitar.
Symbols above reflect actual sounding chords. Capoed fret is "0" in tab.

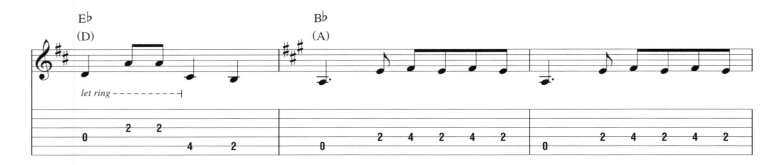

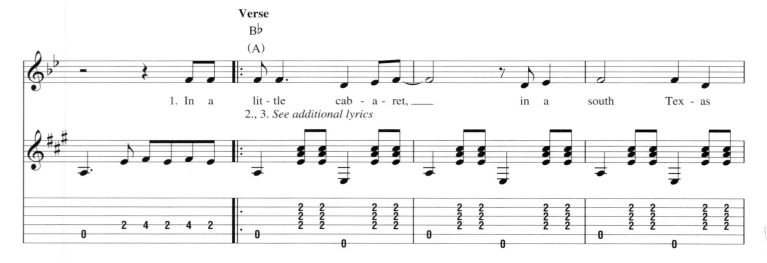

1. In a lit - tle cab - a - ret, ___ in a south Tex - as
2., 3. *See additional lyrics*

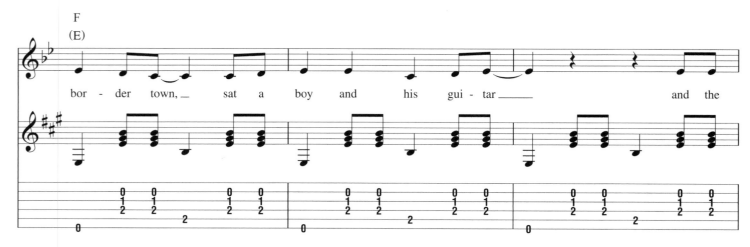

bor - der town, ___ sat a boy and his gui - tar ___ and the

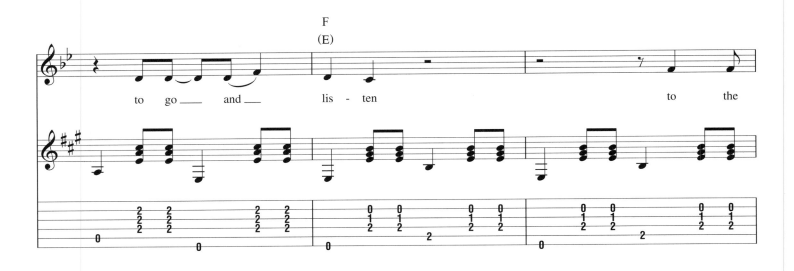

to go ___ and ___ lis - ten to the

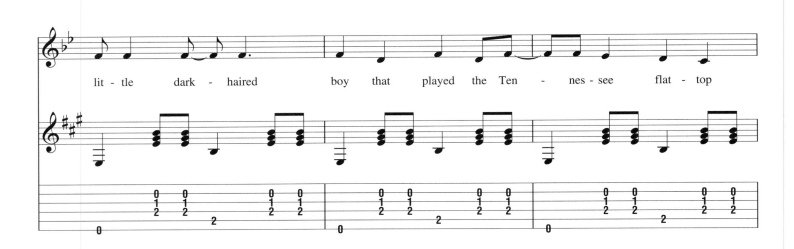

lit - tle dark - haired boy that played the Ten - nes - see flat - top

Guitar Solo

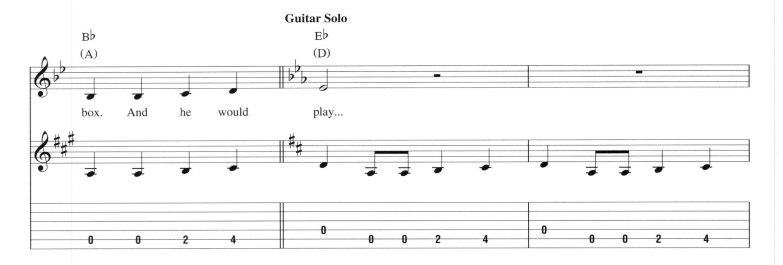

box. And he would play...

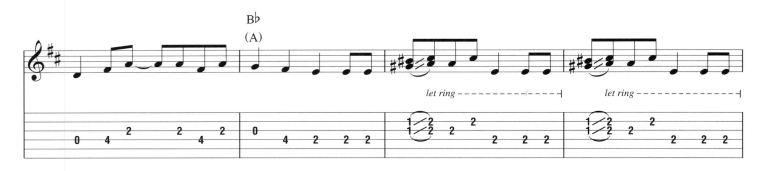

Additional Lyrics

2. Well, he couldn't ride or wrangle and he never cared to make a dime.
   But give him his guitar and he'd be happy all the time.
   And all the girls from nine to ninety
   Were snappin' fingers, tappin' toes and beggin' him, "Don't stop!"
   And hypnotized and fascinated
   By the little dark-haired boy that played the Tennessee flat-top box. And he would play...

3. Then one day he was gone and no one ever saw him 'round.
   He vanished like the breeze and they forgot him in the little town.
   But all the girls still dreamed about him
   And hung around the cabaret until the doors were locked.
   And then one day on the hit parade
   Was a little dark-haired boy that played a Tennessee flat-top box. And he would play...

Guitar Notation Legend

THE MUSICAL STAFF shows pitches and and rhythms and is divided by bar lines into measures. Pitches are named after the first seven letters of the alphabet.

TABLATURE graphically represents the guitar fingerboard. Each horizontal line represents a string, and each number represents a fret.

Notes:

Strings:

4th string, 2nd fret   1st & 2nd strings open, played together   open D chord

HALF-STEP BEND: Strike the note and bend up 1/2 step.

WHOLE-STEP BEND: Strike the note and bend up one step.

GRACE NOTE BEND: Strike the note and bend up as indicated. The first note does not take up any time.

SLIGHT (MICROTONE) BEND: Strike the note and bend up 1/4 step.

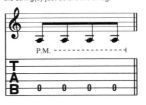

BEND AND RELEASE: Strike the note and bend up as indicated, then release back to the original note. Only the first note is struck.

PRE-BEND: Bend the note as indicated, then strike it.

VIBRATO: The string is vibrated by rapidly bending and releasing the note with the fretting hand.

PALM MUTING: The note is partially muted by the pick hand lightly touching the string(s) just before the bridge.

HAMMER-ON: Strike the first (lower) note with one finger, then sound the higher note (on the same string) with another finger by fretting it without picking.

PULL-OFF: Place both fingers on the notes to be sounded. Strike the first note and without picking, pull the finger off to sound the second (lower) note.

LEGATO SLIDE: Strike the first note and then slide the same fret-hand finger up or down to the second note. The second note is not struck.

SHIFT SLIDE: Same as legato slide, except the second note is struck.

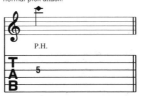

PINCH HARMONIC: The note is fretted normally and a harmonic is produced by adding the edge of the thumb or the tip of the index finger of the pick hand to the normal pick attack.

TRILL: Very rapidly alternate between the notes indicated by continuously hammering on and pulling off.

TAPPING: Hammer ("tap") the fret indicated with the pick-hand index or middle finger and pull off to the note fretted by the fret hand.

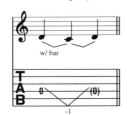

NATURAL HARMONIC: Strike the note while the fret-hand lightly touches the string directly over the fret indicated.

TREMOLO PICKING: The note is picked as rapidly and continuously as possible.

VIBRATO BAR DIVE AND RETURN: The pitch of the note or chord is dropped a specified number of steps (in rhythm) then returned to the original pitch.

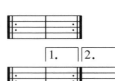

VIBRATO BAR SCOOP: Depress the bar just before striking the note, then quickly release the bar.

VIBRATO BAR DIP: Strike the note and then immediately drop a specified number of steps, then release back to the original pitch.

Additional Musical Definitions

 (accent) • Accentuate note (play it louder)

 (staccato) • Play the note short

Fill • Label used to identify a brief melodic figure which is to be inserted into the arrangement.

N.C. • Instrument is silent (drops out).

D.S. al Coda • Go back to the sign (𝄋), then play until the measure marked *"To Coda"*, then skip to the section labelled *"Coda."*

• Repeat measures between signs.

D.S. al Fine • Go back to the beginning of the song and play until the measure marked *"Fine"* (end).

1. 2. • When a repeated section has different endings, play the first ending only the first time and the second ending only the second time.

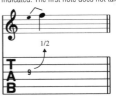

48